REAL-LIFE
SCIENTIFIC
ADVENTURES

HMS *BEAGLE* VOYAGE AND THE GALÁPAGOS ISLANDS

THERESA MORLOCK

PowerKiDS press™

New York

Published in 2019 by The Rosen Publishing Group, Inc.
29 East 21st Street, New York, NY 10010

First Edition

Editor: Theresa Morlock
Book Design: Reann Nye

Photo Credits: Cover, pp.1 SCIENCE PHOTO LIBRARY/Science Photo Library/Getty Images; p. 4 GUDKOV ANDREY/Shutterstock.com; p. 5 (top) dikobraziy/Shutterstock.com; p. 5 (bottom) Jess Kraft/ Shutterstock.com; p. 6 Jolanta Wojcicka/Shutterstock.com; p. 7 (top) SCIENCE SOURCE/Getty Images; p. 7 (bottom) Duba DP/Shutterstock.com; p. 9 (top) jorisvo/Shutterstock.com; p. 9 (bottom) DEA PICTURE LIBRARY/De Agostini/Getty Images; p. 11 https://commons.wikimedia.org/wiki/File:Charles_Darwin_ by_G._Richmond.png; p.12 Olena Tur/Shutterstock.com; p.13 Hulton Archive/Getty Images; p.14 Samuel Borges Photography/Shutterstock.com; p.15 https://commons.wikimedia.org/wiki/File:British_Museum_ Marine_Chronometer.jpg; p.17 (top) Dorling Kindersley/Getty Images; p.17 (bottom) Maurizio De Mattei/ Shutterstock.com; p.18 Discover Marco/Shutterstock.com; p.19 FOTOGRIN/Shutterstock.com; p. 21 (top) https://commons.wikimedia.org/wiki/File:Megatherium_americanum_Skeleton_NHM.JPG; p. 21 (bottom) De Agostini Picture Library/De Agostini/Getty Images; p. 23 Science & Society Picture Library/ SSPL/Getty Images; p. 25 UniversalImagesGroup/Universal Images Group/Getty Images; p. 27 (large ground finch, gray warbler-finch) Stubblefield Photography/Shutterstock.com; p. 27 (small ground finch) Natursports/ Shutterstock.com; p. 27 (mangrove finch) https://commons.wikimedia.org/wiki/File:Camarhynchus_ heliobates.png; p. 27 (medium ground finch) https://commons.wikimedia.org/wiki/File:Geospiza_fortis. jpg; p. 28 Fernando Espinosa/Shutterstock.com; p. 29 (top) Rene Holtslag/Shutterstock.com; p. 29 (bottom) Brendan van Son/Shutterstock.com.

Cataloging-in-Publication Data

Names: Morlock, Theresa.
Title: HMS Beagle voyage and the Galápagos Islands / Theresa Morlock .
Description: New York : PowerKids Press, 2019. | Series: Real-Life scientific adventures | Includes glossary and index.
Identifiers: LCCN ISBN 9781508168485 (pbk.) | ISBN 9781508168461 (library bound) | ISBN 9781508168492 (6 pack)
Subjects: LCSH: Darwin, Charles, 1809-1882–Juvenile literature. | Beagle Expedition (1831-1836)–Juvenile literature. | Galapagos Islands–Juvenile literature.
Classification: LCC QH31.D2 M865 2019 | DDC 508.092–dc23

Manufactured in the United States of America

CPSIA Compliance Information: Batch #CS18PK: For Further Information contact Rosen Publishing, New York, New York at 1-800-237-9932

CONTENTS

A SCIENTIFIC EXPEDITION

A scientific expedition is a journey undertaken by a group of people for a specific scientific purpose. This purpose could be to learn about a faraway place, to discover what kind of geographic features form the

landscape, to research what sorts of plants grow there, or to observe the varying animal species that live there.

The voyage of the HMS *Beagle* was one of the most important scientific expeditions in history. Charles Darwin's investigations as a naturalist aboard the *Beagle* would change how people understood the history of the world and its living things. The trip was sponsored, or paid for, by the British government, which hoped to improve the nation's knowledge of the geography of South America and protect its trade interests there.

The *Galápagos* region was just one of the many places the crew of the *HMS Beagle* explored.

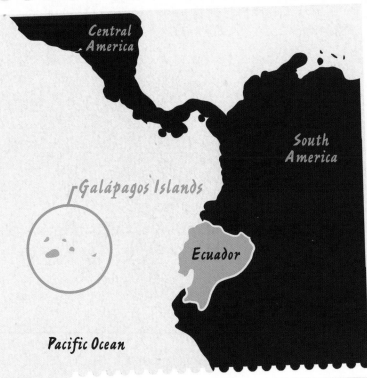

Central America

South America

Galápagos Islands

Ecuador

Pacific Ocean

ABOARD THE HMS BEAGLE

The HMS *Beagle* was a British naval ship. It was the third of nine ships to be named "the *Beagle*." The *Beagle* measured 90 feet, 4 inches (27.5 m) long and 24 feet, 6 inches (7.5 m) across. It was originally a 10-gun brig, which is a kind of ship designed for scouting. It was later expanded.

The first voyage of the HMS *Beagle* began in 1826, under the command of Lieutenant Pringle Stokes. The purpose of the journey was to make scientific observations. These included recording the latitude and longitude of each port of call, observing the tides, ocean currents, and **trade winds**, and mapping out coral reef islands. Careful records were kept about air pressure, temperature, wind, weather, and more.

coral reef

illustration of the HMS Beagle

Atlantic Ocean

THE BEAGLE'S SECOND VOYAGE

Not long after Lieutenant Stokes's death in 1828, Lieutenant Robert Fitzroy became captain of the *Beagle*. Fitzroy identified a new channel through the islands of Tierra del Fuego. He named this the Beagle Channel. In 1830, Fitzroy returned the *Beagle* home to England. He then began preparing for the ship's second voyage.

The purpose of the second voyage of the HMS *Beagle* was to finish the work of the first. The crew would do this by surveying the coastline and charting the harbors of South America.

While organizing the voyage, Captain Fitzroy suggested the need for "a well-educated and scientific person" to help collect useful information during the trip. Professors recommended a young naturalist named Charles Darwin to fill this role.

the *Beagle Channel, Tierra del Fuego* in *Ushuaia, Argentina*

Robert Fitzroy, pictured here, was a scientist as well as a naval officer. He was particularly interested in meteorology, an earth science concerned with the weather.

A YOUNG NATURALIST

Charles Darwin was born in 1809 in Shrewsbury, England. As a young man, he studied medicine at Edinburgh University, Scotland. His education at Edinburgh brought him into contact with many scientists. However, surgery disgusted him. Deciding that medicine wasn't for him, Darwin then attended Cambridge, where he studied to become a minister. At Cambridge, he spent much of his free time collecting and observing beetles.

After his graduation from Cambridge in 1831, Darwin's teacher found him a place on the HMS *Beagle* voyage. Darwin was just 22 years old when he signed on as the ship's naturalist. His job was to collect information

EXPEDITION REPORT

Darwin brought few supplies on the journey. "I have **procured** a case of good strong pistols and an excellent rifle for 50 pounds, there is a saving," he wrote, "a good telescope, with compass, 5 pounds, and these are nearly the only expensive instruments I shall want." Other scientific instruments included a clinometer, which was used for measuring angles. He also brought a Bible.

about the natural history of the places he visited. It was "by far the most important event in my life," Darwin wrote. It "determined my whole career."

11

THE JOURNEY BEGINS

On December 27, 1831, the HMS *Beagle* set sail from Plymouth, England. The plan was to spend two years traveling around the world. In truth, the journey would last almost five years, from December 1831 until October 1836.

Conditions aboard the *Beagle* were very close. The cabin that Darwin shared with two others measured 10 by 11 feet (3.1 by 3.4 m). At night he slept in a hammock two feet from the ceiling. Darwin was very ill aboard the ship. He later wrote:

Tenerife, Canary Islands

EXPEDITION REPORT

Darwin kept a record of all the crew members aboard the *Beagle*. Including himself, there were 76 people on the ship. Among these were first and second lieutenants, a surgeon, a carpenter, two cooks, a rope-maker, and a sailmaker.

While at sea, Darwin spent some of his time reading books such as Principles of Geology by Charles Lyell, pictured here. Lyell's ideas helped shape Darwin's scientific theories.

"The misery I endured from sea-sickness is far beyond what I ever guessed at."

The ship's first stop was planned for January 1832 at Tenerife, one of the Canary Islands. Unfortunately, the crew was not allowed to land due to the fear of spreading illness from England. The ship continued to South America.

On January 16, 1832, the ship landed at Porto Praya on Saint Jago (now Santiago), an island in the Cape Verde archipelago, or chain of islands, off the western coast of Africa. From there, the ship headed west across the Atlantic Ocean. The *Beagle* made its way down the coast of South America, moving past Brazil, Argentina, and the Falkland Islands. The *Beagle* rounded Cape Horn at the southern tip of South America and sailed north up the continent's Pacific coast.

Santiago

EXPEDITION REPORT

It's not easy to keep track of time at sea. During its journey the *Beagle* traveled through different time zones. A marine chronometer is a **unique** kind of clock that measures longitude based on time. Chronometers are specially designed to be exact despite changing temperature and constant motion.

This marine chronometer created by Thomas Earnshaw was used on the HMS Beagle. A chronometer is an instrument that's used to measure time at sea.

Darwin arranged to be dropped off and picked up and spent much of his time on land. While in Brazil, Darwin explored the rain forest. He collected samples to send home. In 1833, Darwin explored the inland of Argentina. He searched for bones and fossils there.

THE GALÁPAGOS

In September 1835, the HMS *Beagle* reached the Galápagos Islands. The Galápagos Islands are located in the Pacific Ocean, about 600 miles (965.6 km) off the coast of Ecuador. There are 19 islands in the Galápagos archipelago. Darwin wrote that there were 10 main islands. Three ocean currents come together in the Galápagos, making it a unique place that's home to hundreds of marine species. The separation of the islands led to the development of unique species such as the land iguana, giant tortoise, and many finches.

Darwin spent 34 days exploring the Galápagos Islands. He collected samples and recorded observations. He also collected fossils. Of the Galápagos region, Darwin said it was "very remarkable: it seems to be a little world within itself; the greater number of its inhabitants, both vegetable and animal, being found nowhere else."

EXPEDITION REPORT

While investigating the Galápagos, Darwin collected **specimens** to send to his friend John Henslow, who had been his professor at Cambridge University. Henslow and Darwin were both interested in the **distribution** of plant and animal species. They studied the links between different species that lived on islands and the mainland of the nearest continent.

This illustration shows Darwin studying a giant tortoise.

land iguana

17

DARWIN'S OBSERVATIONS

While exploring the Galápagos, Darwin observed that the islands differed in terms of climate, landscape, and wildlife. He noted that the islands were formed from volcanic rocks and shaped by **erosion** from the surrounding water. He observed that although the islands were close to the equator, the climate was not uncomfortably hot. He drew the conclusion that the climate was cooled by low water temperature.

EXPEDITION REPORT

Darwin was shocked by the differences between the wildlife on the Galápagos Islands. He wrote: "I never dreamed that islands about **50** or **60** miles (**80.5** to **96.6** km) apart, and most of them in sight of each other, formed of precisely the same rocks, placed under a quite similar climate, rising to a nearly equal height, would have been differently tenanted; but we shall soon see that this is the case."

marine iguanas

This is a Galápagos giant tortoise. They can live for over 100 years and weigh up to 500 pounds (226.8 kg)!

Darwin catalogued many details about the wildlife on the islands. He saw that the tortoises on one island had shells that were shaped differently from those of the tortoises on other islands. He also observed the appearance and behavior of several species of finches. He was curious about the fact that their beaks were different sizes and shapes.

THE REMAINING VOYAGE

Over the course of the journey, Darwin experienced many things that would change the way he understood the world. He saw tropical rain forests with unique animals. This helped him understand the **diversity** of Earth's living creatures. He experienced an earthquake, observed the shapes of landmasses, and saw how conditions shaped landforms. This helped him learn about how processes can change Earth's surface. He saw fossils of extinct animals, such as the giant ground sloth. This taught him that the way animals look can change over time.

After departing the Galápagos, the *Beagle* sailed across the Pacific Ocean to Australia. From Australia the crew headed to Mauritius in the Indian Ocean and then Cape Town, South Africa. They then crossed the Atlantic back to the Brazilian coast. Then, at last, they returned to England.

EXPEDITION REPORT

Darwin reflected on leaving the Galápagos that "It is the fate of most voyagers, no sooner to discover what is most interesting in any locality, than they are hurried from it; but I ought, perhaps, to be thankful that I obtained sufficient materials to establish this most remarkable fact in the distribution of organic beings."

This skeleton of a *Megatherium*, or giant sloth, is kept at the Natural History Museum in London, England. Unlike modern sloths, giant sloths could be as large as elephants!

Illustration of a
Megatherium

THE VOYAGE OF THE BEAGLE

When the *Beagle* returned to England in October 1836, Darwin had sailed 40,000 miles (64,373.8 km) around the world. He collected over 5,000 specimens. He explored 2,000 miles (3,218.7 km) inland. The specimens included over 1,500 different species, hundreds of which had never been seen in Europe.

After the expedition was completed, Captain Fitzroy wrote an account of what he had experienced. He called it **Narrative** of the Surveying Voyages of HMS Adventure and Beagle. Fitzroy asked Darwin to contribute to the account, which would be published in three volumes. The narrative was published in 1839. Darwin's contribution, which made up the third volume, would later be renamed *The Voyage of the Beagle*. While writing, Darwin reflected on what he had seen and formed his theory of evolution by natural selection.

Darwin also acted as an editor to this book by Richard Owen, founder of the Natural History Museum in London.

THE

ZOOLOGY

OF

THE VOYAGE OF H.M.S. BEAGLE,

UNDER THE COMMAND OF CAPTAIN FITZROY, R.N.,

DURING THE YEARS

1832 TO 1836.

PUBLISHED WITH THE APPROVAL OF
THE LORDS COMMISSIONERS OF HER MAJESTY'S TREASURY.

Edited and Superintended by

CHARLES DARWIN, ESQ. M.A. F.R.S. SEC. G.S.

NATURALIST TO THE EXPEDITION.

PART I.

FOSSIL MAMMALIA:

BY

RICHARD OWEN, ESQ. F.R.S.

PROFESSOR OF ANATOMY AND PHYSIOLOGY TO THE ROYAL COLLEGE OF SURGEONS IN LONDON;
CORRESPONDING MEMBER OF THE INSTITUTE OF FRANCE, ETC. ETC.

LONDON:

PUBLISHED BY SMITH, ELDER AND CO. 65, CORNHILL.

MDCCCXL.

23

THE THEORY OF EVOLUTION

Evolution is the process by which living organisms change over time. In 1859, Darwin published *On the Origin of Species*. In it he discussed his ideas about the theory of evolution based on what he had learned in the Galápagos Islands.

He wrote: "When on board HMS *Beagle*, as naturalist, I was much struck with certain facts." Darwin described how the Galápagos Islands shared similar **environments**, but there were differences between the creatures living there. Why did the finches on the different islands have beaks of different sizes and shapes? He concluded that the finches had adapted to suit their local environments. The Galápagos finches had developed unique beaks over time because they adapted to eating the seeds or insects that were native to the island they lived on.

24

These illustrations show some of the different finches that Darwin observed in the Galápagos Islands.

NATURAL SELECTION

Darwin's theory of evolution is based on the idea of natural selection. Natural selection means that living things with beneficial **traits** tend to survive to produce offspring. It's sometimes referred to as "survival of the fittest." The members of a species with the most beneficial traits more often pass on those traits to the next generation. Evolution occurs in part because of natural selection. As beneficial traits are passed on from generation to generation, a species changes and develops.

Darwin's ideas about evolution by natural selection were shocking to many people. At that time, most people believed that all plant and animal species were made at one time. Darwin proved that all living things weren't created at once, but evolved over time. All of Earth's living species evolved from earlier species.

large ground finch

mangrove finch

grey warbler-finch

medium ground finch

There are 13 species of Galápagos finches. Each evolved from one common ancestor.

27

THE GALÁPAGOS TODAY

The HMS *Beagle* expedition changed the world in an unexpected way. In the Galápagos, Darwin collected evidence that he later recognized as proof of evolution by natural selection. For many years, Darwin hesitated to publish his findings. He knew that his ideas would anger many people who faithfully believed that all species were created at one time. His experiences and observations as the ship's naturalist and his time on the Galápagos Islands led him to scientific conclusions that would permanently transform the way people understood life on Earth and their place in the world. Many resisted these new ideas because they found them threatening.

Today the Galápagos Islands are protected as a World **Heritage** site. They are considered one of the most historically and scientifically important places on the planet.

Today, the Galápagos Islands are a popular place to visit.

Galápagos sea lions

Journey to the Galápagos

December 27, 1831
The *Beagle* departs Plymouth, England.

January 6, 1832
The *Beagle* reaches the Canary Islands, but the crew can't go ashore.

January 16, 1832
The *Beagle* reaches the Cape Verde Islands.

March 1832
Darwin explores Brazilian rain forests.

April 1832
Darwin treks 150 miles inland to Rio de Janeiro.

September 1832
The *Beagle* reaches Punta Alta, Argentina.

December 1832
The *Beagle* reaches Tierra del Fuego. Captain Fitzroy releases three native people he'd taken to England on a previous voyage.

March 1835
Darwin climbs the Andes Mountains in Valparaíso, Chile.

September–October 1835
Darwin studies plants, birds, and animals on the Galápagos Islands.

January 1836
Darwin studies animals in Sydney, Australia.

April 1836
Darwin studies coral islands in the Cocos Islands.

April 1836
The *Beagle* reaches Mauritius in the Indian Ocean.

May–June 1836
The *Beagle* reaches Cape Town, South Africa, where Darwin visits astronomer John Herschel.

August 1836
The *Beagle* arrives at Bahia, Brazil.

October 2, 1836
Darwin returns to Falmouth, England.

GLOSSARY

distribution: Having to do with the way something is shared or spread out.

diversity: The quality or state of having many different types, forms, or ideas.

environment: The conditions that surround a living thing and affect the way it lives.

erosion: The wearing away of the earth's surface by wind or water.

heritage: The traditions and beliefs that are part of the history of a group or nation.

narrative: A story.

procure: To get possession of something.

specimen: A scientific sample of something, or an individual considered usual for a group.

trade winds: A wind blowing almost constantly toward the equator from the northeast.

trait: A quality that makes one person or thing different from another.

unique: Special or different from anything else.

INDEX

WEBSITES

Due to the changing nature of Internet links, PowerKids Press has developed an online list of websites related to the subject of this book. This site is updated regularly. Please use this link to access the list: www.powerkidslinks.com/rlsa/beagle